| LEWISHAM LIBRARY SERVICE | |
| --- | --- |
| Askews & Holts | 25-Mar-2016 |
| J510 JUNIOR NON-FICT | 7J |
| | |

# [A Maths] JOURNEY <=~±÷ ›around the‹ Wonders of the World

WAYLAND
www.waylandbooks.co.uk

# CONTENTS

**04** THE PYRAMIDS OF EGYPT

**06** THE TAJ MAHAL

**08** WATERFALLS OF THE WORLD

**10** THE GREAT WALL OF CHINA

**12** THE TERRACOTTA ARMY

**14** THE AMAZON

**16** ANTARCTICA

**18** THE ACROPOLIS

**20** BURJ KHALIFA

**22** MOUNT EVEREST

**24** STONEHENGE

**26** GALÁPAGOS

**28** GO FIGURE! ANSWERS

**30** MATHS GLOSSARY

**32** INDEX

# go figure

Get ready for the trip of a lifetime as you use your mathematical skills to collect information for a travel guide to the wonders of the world.

## LEARN ABOUT IT
### NEGATIVE NUMBERS

This section will take you through the mathematical ideas you'll need to complete each mission.

The practical examples in this section will test your knowledge of the ideas you've just learnt.

## >GO FIGURE!

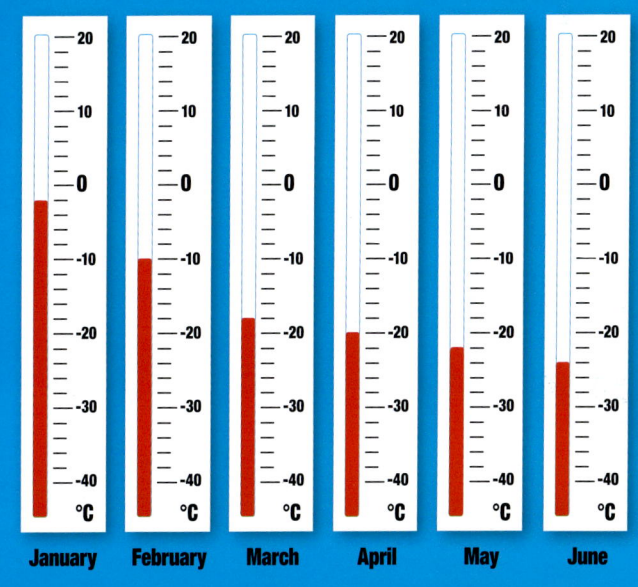

January  February  March  April  May  June

## ANSWERS AND GLOSSARY

Answers to the Go Figure! challenges can be found on page 28. Words in *italics* appear in the glossary on page 30.

You might find some of the questions in this book are too hard to do without the help of a calculator. Ask your teacher about when and how to use a calculator.

## WHAT EQUIPMENT DO YOU NEED?

Pen or pencil     Notepad

## MISSION 1

# THE PYRAMIDS OF EGYPT

Your first mission takes you to Egypt. Here, three giant stone *pyramids* were built more than 3000 years ago. They still tower above the desert sands. Your task is to work out their sizes.

### LEARN ABOUT IT
### PYRAMIDS, NETS AND SURFACE AREAS

A pyramid is a 3D shape with a base and triangular faces. A square-based pyramid has a square base and four triangular faces. The top point of the pyramid is called its apex.

A net is a flat pattern that is folded to make a 3D shape. The net of a square-based pyramid has four triangles and a square joined together. They can be joined in different ways. This is just one example:

To find the *area* of a rectangle, multiply the length by the width, so to find the area of a square, multiply the length by itself. To find the area of a triangle, multiply the length of the base (b) by the perpendicular height (h) and halve the answer. This can be given as the formula:

**area of a triangle = ½b x h**

To find the surface area of a pyramid, find the area of each part of the net and add them together.

# ›GO FIGURE!

You need to find out the sizes of the pyramids so that you can give the information in your travel guide. The largest is the Great Pyramid, the second largest is the Second Pyramid and the smallest is the Third Pyramid.

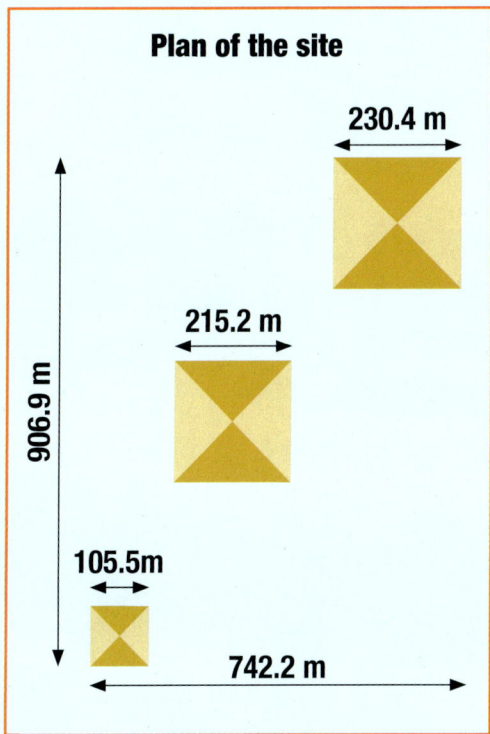

**Plan of the site**

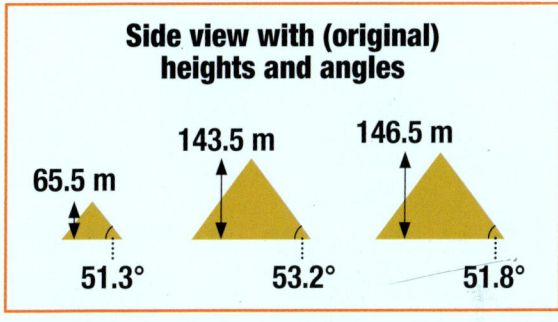

**Side view with (original) heights and angles**

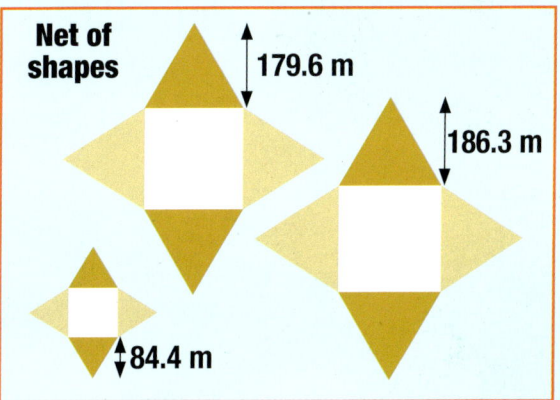

**Net of shapes**

① For each pyramid, find the area of the square base.

② **The height of the Great Pyramid has decreased since it was built due to erosion. It is now 7.7 m shorter. What is its current height?**

③ Using the original heights shown above, how much taller was the Second Pyramid than the Third Pyramid?

④ **For each of the pyramids, find the surface area of the whole 3D shape.**

05

## MISSION 2

# THE TAJ MAHAL

Your next mission takes you to India to report on the beautiful architecture of the Taj Mahal, including its reflection pool.

### LEARN ABOUT IT
### TRANSFORMATIONS AND SYMMETRY

**Transformations** are ways of changing geometric shapes. They include reflection, rotation and translation. These three transformations do not change the size or angles of the shapes.

Reflections are made in a mirror line.

Rotations are made about a point through different amounts of turn and in different directions. Here the turns are 90° clockwise.

Translations are when you slide a shape without turning or reflecting it. You can translate a shape horizontally, vertically or diagonally.

06

Shapes can have many lines of reflective *symmetry*. Regular shapes have the same number of *lines of symmetry* as the number of sides. They can also have rotational symmetry, which describes the number of times the shape can be turned and will fit into its own outline.

| Shape | Number of lines of reflective symmetry | Order of rotational symmetry |
|---|---|---|
| L | 0 | 1 |
| ♥ | 1 | 1 |
| ⬟ | 5 | 5 |

# ›GO FIGURE!

For this section of the travel guide, you need to describe the amazing patterns, symmetries and geometric shapes found in the Taj Mahal. Study these photos from your travel guide.

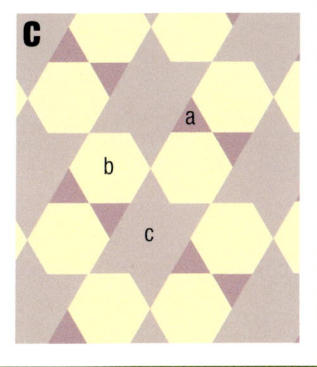

**1.** How many lines of reflective symmetry does photo A show?

**2.** The repeating pattern in photo B shows how many full translations?

**3.** Photo C shows a tile pattern made from three different shapes: a: equilateral triangles, b: regular hexagons and c: another shape. What is shape c? Use the word regular or irregular in your answer.

**4.** In total, how many lines of symmetry do each of the shapes a, b and c have?

**5.** In the fourth photo are lawns shaped like this diagram. Describe the shape in terms of its number of sides, and its number of lines of reflective and rotational symmetry. How many right angles and other angles does it have?

07

## MISSION 3: WATERFALLS OF THE WORLD

You want to include one of the world's major waterfalls in your guide, but you can't decide which one. So you'll need to gather lots of information and compare the data.

### LEARN ABOUT IT: COMPARING AND ROUNDING NUMBERS

**When comparing numbers it is important to know the values of the digits.**

To order 39,904, 42,692, 9986 and 42,357 from largest to smallest, as shown below, line up the digits in the correct columns and compare them from left to right. If two digits are the same, compare the digits to their right and so on.

| Ten thousands | Thousands | Hundreds | Tens | Units |
|---|---|---|---|---|
| 4 | 2 | 6 | 9 | 2 |
| 4 | 2 | 3 | 5 | 7 |
| 3 | 9 | 9 | 0 | 4 |
|   | 9 | 9 | 8 | 6 |

### Rounding

- **To the nearest 10**
If the Units digit is 5 or more, the Tens digit goes up one, otherwise it stays the same. Units digit becomes zero.

- **To the nearest 100**
If the Tens digit is 5 or more, the Hundreds digit goes up one. Tens and Units digits become zero.

- **To the nearest 1000**
If the Hundreds digit is 5 or more, the Thousands digit goes up one. Hundreds, Tens and Units digits become zero.

| Number | Rounded to the nearest 10 | Rounded to the nearest 100 | Rounded to the nearest 1000 |
|---|---|---|---|
| 5829 | 5830 | 5800 | 6000 |
| 23,687 | 23,690 | 23,700 | 24,000 |
| 18,009 | 18,010 | 18,000 | 18,000 |

# >GO FIGURE!

On your travels, you have collected information on five waterfalls from South America, North America and Africa. The information recorded includes height, width, average flow rate over a year, and the number of different levels the water flows over.

| Name | Countries | Height (m) | Mean annual flow rate (m³/s) | Width (m) | Tallest single level (m) | Total number of levels |
|---|---|---|---|---|---|---|
| Angel Falls | Bolivia/Venezuela | 979 | 14 | 107 | 807 | 2 |
| Iguazu Falls | Brazil/Argentina | 82 | 1756 | 2682 | 82 | 275 |
| Kaieteur Falls | Guyana | 226 | 663 | 113 | 226 | 1 |
| Niagara Falls | US/Canada | 51 | 2407 | 1203 | 51 | 3 |
| Victoria Falls | Zimbabwe/Zambia | 108 | 1088 | 1708 | 108 | 1 |

**1** Which falls have: a) the greatest height? b) the largest flow rate? c) the greatest width?

**2** a) Write the height of each of the falls to the nearest 10 m. b) Write the widths to the nearest 100 m.

**3** On average, how many m³ of water flow each minute (60 seconds) at: a) Iguazu? b) Niagara?

**4** Give points 1 to 5 to each fall according to their height, flow rate and width, with 5 points for the largest number in each category. How many points does each of the falls score? Which of the falls wins? Would it still win if you included points in the same way for the last two columns as well?

09

## MISSION 4: THE GREAT WALL OF CHINA

To visit the next two wonders of the world, you must travel to China, a country full of exotic places. Here you'll find the Great Wall of China, a structure thousands of kilometres long.

### LEARN ABOUT IT: LARGE NUMBERS

When describing large numbers we group the digits in threes, which we often mark using a comma or a space e.g. 473,695 or 473 695.

In 26,789, the 26 stands for 'thousands' so it is 'twenty-six thousand, seven hundred and eighty nine'.

| Billions ||| Millions ||| Thousands ||| Ones |||
|---|---|---|---|---|---|---|---|---|---|---|---|
| HB | TB | B | HM | TM | M | HTh | TTh | Th | H | T | U |
|  |  |  |  |  |  |  | 2 | 6 | 7 | 8 | 9 |

In 55,031,044, the 55 stands for '*millions*' and the 031 stands for 'thousands' so it is 'fifty-five million, thirty-one thousand, and forty four'.

| Billions ||| Millions ||| Thousands ||| Ones |||
|---|---|---|---|---|---|---|---|---|---|---|---|
| HB | TB | B | HM | TM | M | HTh | TTh | Th | H | T | U |
|  |  |  |  | 5 | 5 | 0 | 3 | 1 | 0 | 4 | 4 |

In 2,104,030,001, the 2 stands for '*billions*', the 104 stands for 'millions' and the 030 stands for 'thousands', so it is 'two billion, one hundred and four million, thirty thousand, and one'.

| Billions ||| Millions ||| Thousands ||| Ones |||
|---|---|---|---|---|---|---|---|---|---|---|---|
| HB | TB | B | HM | TM | M | HTh | TTh | Th | H | T | U |
|  |  | 2 | 1 | 0 | 4 | 0 | 3 | 0 | 0 | 0 | 1 |

Numbers can also be described in thousands, millions or billions like this:

5,000,000 **5 million**
5,600,000 **5.6 million**
800,000 **800 thousand or 0.8 million**
400,000,000 **400 million or 0.4 billion**
1,300,000,000 **1.3 billion**

# ⟩GO FIGURE!

For your travel guide you must provide information on the size of the Great Wall and facts and figures relating to the numbers of tourists.

**1)** Write in words: a) the official length of the Great Wall, b) the circumference of the equator, c) the *estimated* total length of the different parts of the wall.

**2)** **Write in millions, the number of overseas visitors to China in: a) 2014 b) 2013 c) 2012**

**3)** Using the estimate for the number of visitors to the Great Wall each year, find an estimate for the number of visitors over 10 years. Give your answer: a) in words b) in figures c) in millions d) in billions

The official length of the Great Wall is 8850 km, made up of 6259 km sections of wall, 359 km of trenches and 2232 km of natural barriers such as hills and rivers. The walls are around 8 m wide and range from 5 m to 8 m tall.

Including all the different branches of the Great Wall, it is estimated at 21,196 km long, which is more than half the distance around the Equator (the circumference of the Equator is 40,075 km).

This table shows the number of tourists coming from overseas to visit China in recent years

| Year | Number of overseas visitors |
|------|------------------------------|
| 2014 | 26,360,800 |
| 2013 | 26,290,300 |
| 2012 | 27,191,600 |

The Great Wall receives an estimated 10.72 million visitors each year.

11

# MISSION 5

# THE TERRACOTTA ARMY

While in China, you can visit the amazing Terracotta Army – rows of 8000 life-size statues of warriors and their horses uncovered in an ancient imperial tomb. Every statue has a different facial expression.

## LEARN ABOUT IT
### LONG MULTIPLICATION AND AREA

To do long multiplication, you need to know short multiplication (example 1). You also need to know how to multiply by a multiple of 10, by putting a zero in the units column and then multiplying by the tens digit (example 2).

```
   746
 ×   4
  ----
  2984
  2 1 2
```
example 1

```
   746
 ×  40
  -----
 29840
  2 1 2
```
example 2

In long multiplication, you multiply the number by the units digit and then by the multiple of 10 and add the answers. Here are a couple of examples:

```
     251
   ×  36
    ----
    1506    251 × 6
        1 3
  + 7530    251 × 30
    ----
    9036
       1
```

```
     984
   ×  73
    ----
    2952    984 × 3
       2 2 1
  +68880    984 × 70
    -----
   71832
      5 2
   1 1 1
```

The example to the right shows how to divide 84,690 by 6, using short division. Work from left to right when dividing in this way.

$$6\overline{)84^26^390}  = 14115$$

# ›GO FIGURE!

You are reporting on the number of terracotta soldiers and the size of each vault.

Excavation of more than 1500 statues is still going on

68 figures, four horses and a wooden chariot excavated

**Vault 2**
Crossbowmen, charioteers and cavalry
Size of vault: 94 m × 84 m

**Vault 3**
The officers
Size of vault: 21 m × 17 m

**Vault 1**
The main army (infantry)
Size of vault: 210 m × 62 m

One quarter of the area has been excavated, revealing more than 1500 statues (out of an estimated 6000)

**1** In Vault 1 there are three rows at the front with 68 soldiers in each row. How many soldiers is this?

**2** There are also 9 trenches, each with 36 rows of four soldiers. How many soldiers is this?

**3** Use long multiplication to find, in m², the area of: a) Vault 3 b) Vault 2 c) Vault 1

**4** Use short division to find one quarter of the area of Vault 1 to show the area that has been excavated.

## MISSION 6: THE AMAZON

Your next mission takes you to South America to the mighty Amazon River and rainforest. Packed with wildlife, the huge rainforest covers a larger area than the rest of the world's rainforests put together.

### LEARN ABOUT IT: HECTARES AND MULTIPLYING BY 100

Areas of land are often measured in *hectares*. One hectare is equal to 10,000 m$^2$, which is the area of a 100 m by 100 m square.

A full-sized football pitch is a bit smaller than one hectare.

The area of 1 km by 1 km square (which is 1 km$^2$) is equal to 100 hectares: 1 km$^2$ = 100 hectares.

To multiply a number by 100, move the digits of the number two places to the left.

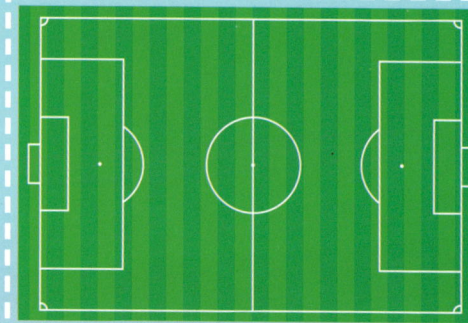

1 hectare

| Millions ||| Thousands ||| Ones |||  |
| HM | TM | M | HTh | TTh | Th | H | T | U |  |
|---|---|---|---|---|---|---|---|---|---|
|  |  | 5 | 5 | 0 | 0 | 0 | 0 | 0 | ×100 |
| 5 | 5 | 0 | 0 | 0 | 0 | 0 | 0 | 0 |  |
|  |  | 1 | 2 | 2 | 5 | 8 | 0 | 0 | ×100 |
| 1 | 2 | 2 | 5 | 8 | 0 | 0 | 0 | 0 |  |

The area of the Amazon rainforest is 5.5 million km²

5,500,000 km² = 550,000,000 hectares, which is 550 million hectares.

Similarly an area of 1,225,600 km² = 122,560,000 hectares which is 122.56 million hectares.

# ⟩GO FIGURE!

The rainforest is under constant threat of deforestation by loggers and farmers. You must report on how much has been deforested and whether the rate has increased or decreased.

*The table shows the average number of km² of Amazon rainforest destroyed in Brazil between 1988 and 2014.*

| Period of time (9 year periods) | 1988–1996 | 1997–2005 | 2006–2014 |
|---|---|---|---|
| Average area of land deforested each year | 17,400 km² | 19,400 km² | 8600 km² |

**1** From 1988–1996, how many km² of land was destroyed in total over the 9 year period?

**2** How much more land was deforested each year during the 1997–2005 period than in 1988–1996 period? Give your answer in hectares.

**3** How much less land was deforested each year during the 2006–2014 period than in 1997–2005 period? Give your answer in hectares and also as the number of million hectares.

**4** Calculate the total amount of land deforested from 1988 to 2014. Give your answer as the number of million hectares.

15

**MISSION 7**

# ANTARCTICA

The next part of your journey takes you on a cruise past the towering icebergs of Antarctica, the coldest place on Earth. Due to its extreme temperatures, tourists visit only in summer between November and March.

### LEARN ABOUT IT
### NEGATIVE NUMBERS AND TEMPERATURE

Temperatures are a good example of *positive* and *negative numbers*. Negative numbers are numbers that are less than zero. Positive numbers are numbers that are greater than zero.

On this thermometer, the negative temperatures, such as -8°C (minus eight degrees Celsius), are below zero and positive temperatures are above zero. Zero or 0°C is the temperature at which water freezes.

To find how much colder one temperature is than another, count down from the smaller number to the larger number.

-20°C is 12 degrees colder than -8°C

16

# ›GO FIGURE!

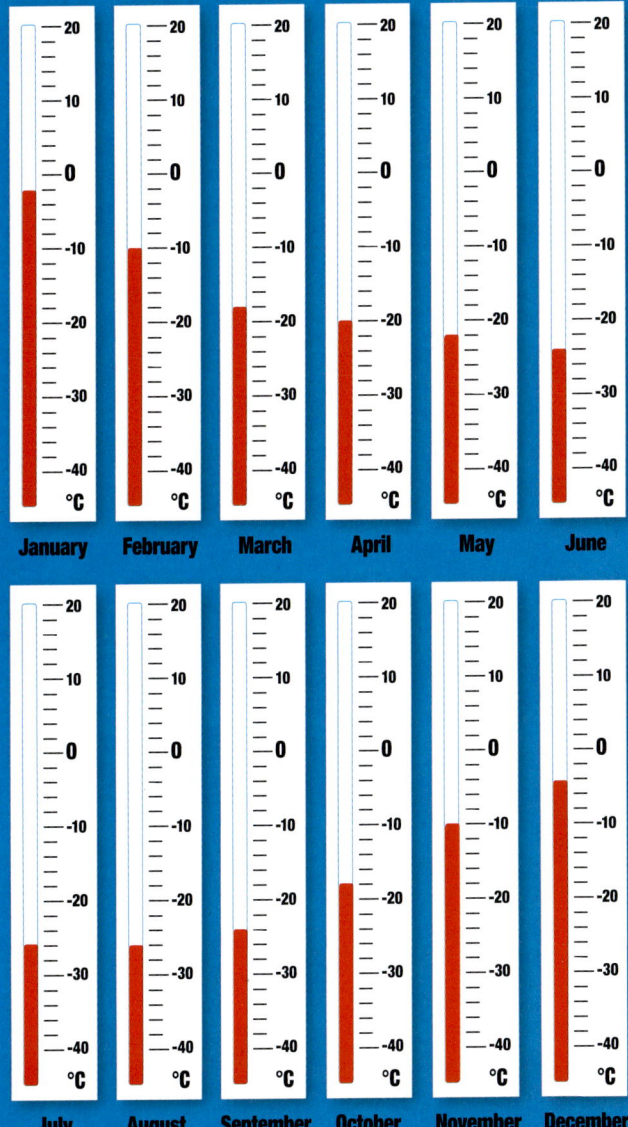

Find out about expected temperatures at different times of year to provide information for your travel guide. These thermometers show the mean average temperatures in each month at one location on the coast of Antarctica.

**1** What is the mean temperature in: a) November? b) January? c) May d) July?

**2** Which is the warmest month?

**3** How much colder is it in: a) September than in February? b) March than November?

**4** Find the mean average temperature over the whole year by adding each reading and dividing the answer by 12.

## MISSION 8

# THE ACROPOLIS

In Athens, Greece, you must gather information on the mathematical dimensions of the Parthenon, the famous temple overlooking the city.

### LEARN ABOUT IT
### GOLDEN RATIO AND GOLDEN RECTANGLES

**Mathematicians have discovered a special number that occurs in nature and in geometry called *Phi*, written as φ.**

Phi is approximately 1.6180339887498948482045868340… and can be written exactly using the formula $\frac{1+\sqrt{5}}{2}$

The *ratio* of 1:φ or 1:1.618… is known as the Golden Ratio. It is found in lots of places and can best be shown as a rectangle with the width representing 1 and the length being 1.618… times greater.

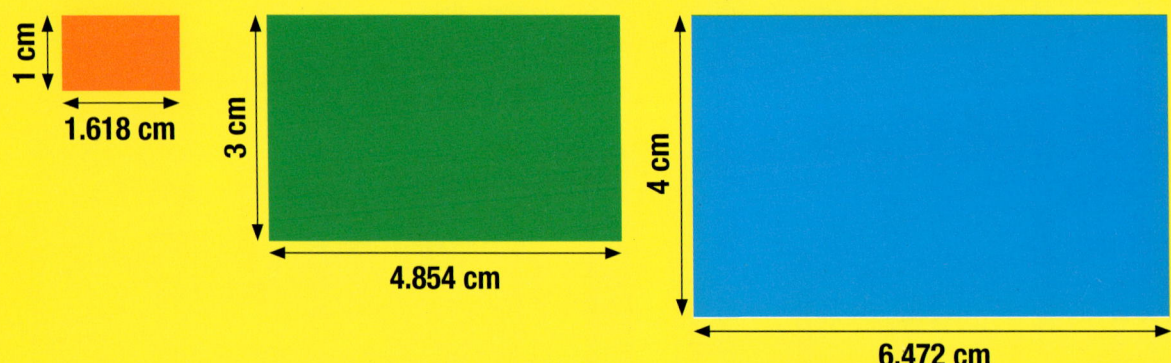

Each of these rectangles has sides in the same ratio as the Golden Ratio. They are called Golden Rectangles. They can be repeatedly drawn to form patterns, seen in nature, in art and in architecture.

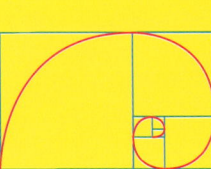

# ⟩GO FIGURE!

You visit the Parthenon to measure the length of the base of the rectangle at the front of it and find that it is 30 metres across.

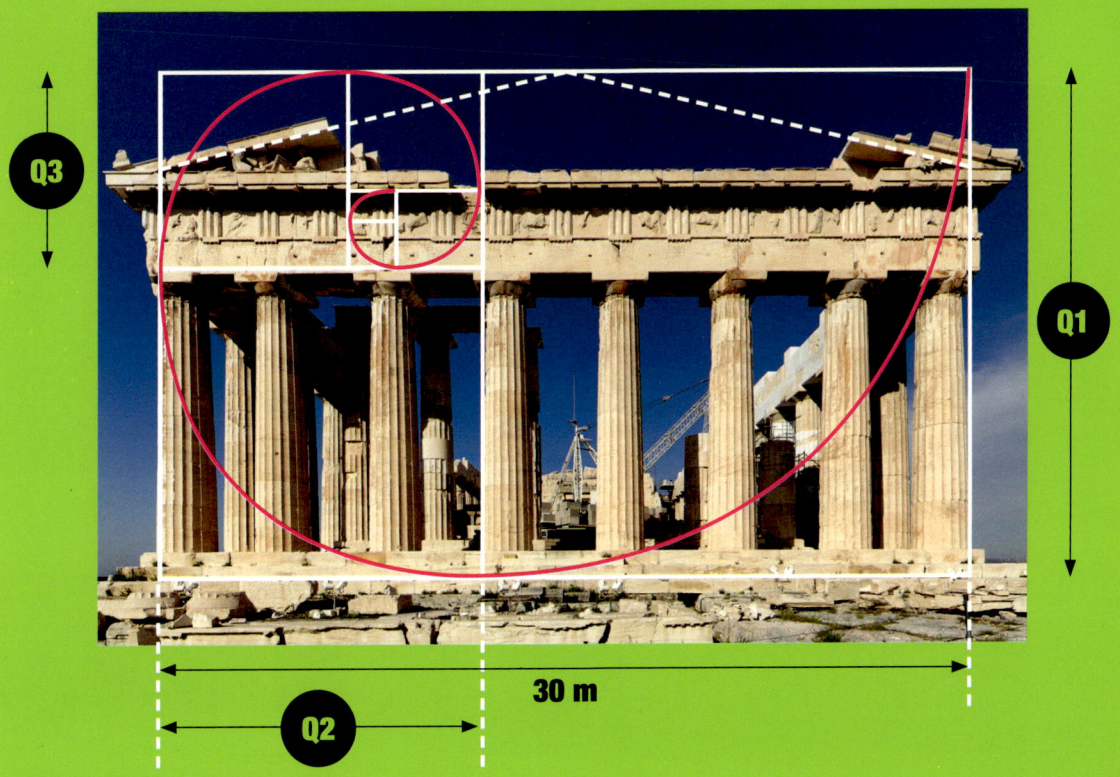

1. Use a calculator to work out an approximate height of the roof by dividing 30 m by the number φ.

2. Divide your answer to question 1 by φ to find the distance from the first to the fourth pillars.

3. Divide your answer to question 2 by φ to find the distance from the top of the pillars to the top of the original roof.

Round each of your answers to 1 decimal place.

MISSION 9

# BURJ KHALIFA

The world's largest skyscraper, the Burj Khalifa, towers above Dubai. Use *algebra* to uncover some fascinating facts about it.

**LEARN ABOUT IT**
**ALGEBRA AND FORMULAE**

**An algebraic formula is a short way of showing relationships between two or more things. Formulae usually use letters to stand for the different things.**

$$T = n \times l$$

is a formula for finding T, the total length of water pipes needed for a skyscraper, when given n, the number of floors of a skyscraper, and l, the length of pipes needed for each floor. We can substitute two numbers into the formula to find the third.

So, if n is 20 floors and l is 615 m we can find the total:

$$T = 20 \times 615 = 12{,}300 \text{ m}$$

or 12.3 km of water pipes.

The time, t, a lift takes to travel a particular distance, d, given a particular speed, s, can be shown by the formula:

$$t = d \div s \quad \text{or} \quad t = d/s$$

20

The time it would take a lift to go a distance of 78 m travelling at a speed of 6 m/s is:

$$t = 78 \div 6 = 13 \text{ seconds}$$

Another formula allows us to change temperatures given in degrees Fahrenheit, F, to degrees Celsius, C.

$$\tfrac{5}{9}(F - 32) = C$$

## ⟩GO FIGURE!

Discover facts about the Burj Khalifa and use the formulae to find out more.

- The outside temperature at the top of the tower is 68°F on the day you arrive.
- The Burj Khalifa in Dubai is 828 m tall.
- The floor area is 309,473 m².
- It has 163 floors that contain offices and 1044 residential apartments.
- There are 57 lifts, the main service lift rises 504 m.
- The outside of the building is covered with 28,261 glass panels.
- The Burj Khalifa's water system supplies an average of 946,000 l per day.

**1** Using the formula $T = n \times l$ find the total length of water pipes when $n = 163$ floors and $l = 615$ m. Give your answer first in metres and then in kilometres.

**2** Use the formula $t = d \div s$ to find how long it would take to travel up 504 m in the lift, moving at an average speed of:
a) 6 m/s   b) 8 m/s
Give your answers in minutes and seconds.

**3** What is the temperature at the top in degrees Celsius (°C) on the day you arrive?

## MISSION 10

# MOUNT EVEREST

The highest wonder, Mount Everest, soars about 8850 m above sea level. Climb to the top, using fractions and percentages to plan your mission.

### LEARN ABOUT IT
**FRACTIONS AND PERCENTAGES**

**Parts of a whole can be expressed as fractions by putting the part on top of the fraction and the whole on the bottom.**

For example, if you walked 2000 m out of a total of 8000 m this can be written as the fraction:

$$\frac{2000}{8000}$$

Fractions can then be written in their simplest form by dividing both numbers by their largest *factor*. Here both numbers can be divided by 2000 to give the fraction ¼:

$$\frac{2000}{8000} \xrightarrow{\div 2000}_{\div 2000} = \frac{1}{4}$$

Sometimes it is easier to divide several times to reach the simplest form.

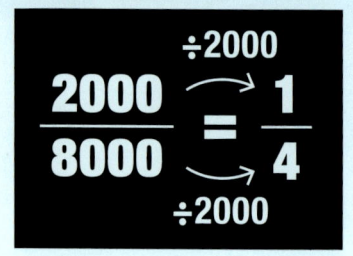

$$\frac{77}{140} \xrightarrow{\div 7}_{\div 7} = \frac{11}{20}$$

$$\frac{3540}{8850} \xrightarrow{\div 10}_{\div 10} = \frac{354}{885} \xrightarrow{\div 3}_{\div 3} = \frac{118}{295} \xrightarrow{\div 59}_{\div 59} = \frac{2}{5}$$

Fractions can also be expressed as *percentages*. To write a fraction as a percentage, where the denominator (the bottom number) is a factor of 100, find what you must multiply it by to get 100. Then multiply both numbers by it.

The percentage is the top number of the answer. Here are some examples:

$$\frac{1}{4} \xrightarrow{\times 25} \frac{25}{100} = 25\%$$

$$\frac{11}{20} \xrightarrow{\times 5} \frac{55}{100} = 55\%$$

It is useful to learn the percentage equivalents of one third and two thirds also:

$$\frac{1}{3} = 33.33\% \qquad \frac{2}{3} = 66.67\%$$

## > GO FIGURE!

At various points up Mount Everest, the camps provide safe places to rest on your journey to the summit. You'll need to give information in your guide about what proportion of the way up these and other points of interest are.

Summit: 8850 m
Camp 4: 8260 m — 1.25 km
Camp 3: 7900 m — 0.75 km
Camp 2: 7670 m — 0.5 km
— 1.5 km
Camp 1: 7080 m
— 2 km
Advanced Base Camp: 6600 m
— 9 km
Interim Base Camp: 5900 m
— 9 km
Base Camp: 5310 m

Give your answers to these questions in their simplest form.

**1** What fraction of the height of Everest is:
a) Base Camp? b) Interim Base Camp?
c) Camp 1? d) Camp 2? e) Camp 4?

**2** Write each of these as a percentage of the height of Everest: a) Base Camp b) Interim Base Camp c) Camp 1 d) Camp 2

**3** The walk from Base Camp to the summit is 24 km in total. What fraction of this distance is the walk from:
a) Base Camp to Interim Base Camp?
b) Advanced Base Camp to Camp 1?
c) Camp 1 to the Summit?
d) Advanced Base Camp to the Summit?

**4** Write the proportion of 24 km represented by the walk from Advanced Base Camp to the Summit as a percentage.

23

## MISSION 11: STONEHENGE

The prehistoric monument of Stonehenge, in England, is made up of circles of giant stones. For your mission, measure them and include their dimensions in your guide.

### LEARN ABOUT IT: CIRCLES AND MEASUREMENTS

The *radius* of a circle is the distance from the edge to its centre. It is half the size of the *diameter*, which is the widest distance across the circle, through the centre.

The *circumference* is the distance all the way around the outside of the circle. It is another word for the *perimeter* of the circle.

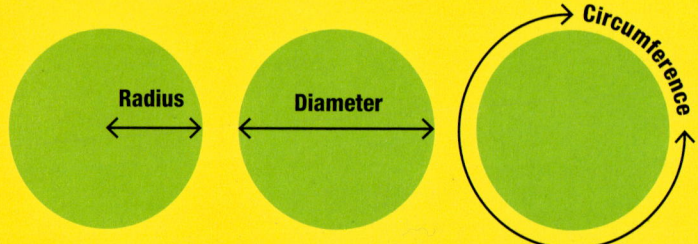

There is a special relationship between the diameter of a circle and its circumference. For every circle, the circumference will always be 3.1412… times the length of the diameter. We call this number *pi* and write it like this: π. The fraction 22/7 is sometimes used as an estimate for pi.

We can write this as C = π × d or even use the radius (which is half the diameter) to give C = π × r x 2. These are often written without the multiplication signs as:

**C = πd**

and

**C = 2πr**

We can use pi to find the area of a circle using the formula Area = π × radius × radius, which is usually written as:

$$A = \pi r^2$$

## >GO FIGURE!

At Stonehenge, you learn about the different circles making up the ancient monument, as shown on this diagram. The table below gives the approximate radius of each circle.

| Name | radius |
|---|---|
| Outer Chalk Bank | 56 m |
| Inner Chalk Bank | 45.5 m |
| Aubrey Circle of Holes | 44 m |
| Circle of "Y" Holes | 27.5 m |
| Circle of "Z" Holes | 20 m |
| Exterior of the Sarsen Circle | 16.5 m |
| Interior of the Sarsen Circle | 15.4 m |
| Outer Bluestone Circle | 12.1 m |
| Great Trilithon Horseshoe | 7.7 m |
| Inner Bluestones Horseshoe | 6 m |

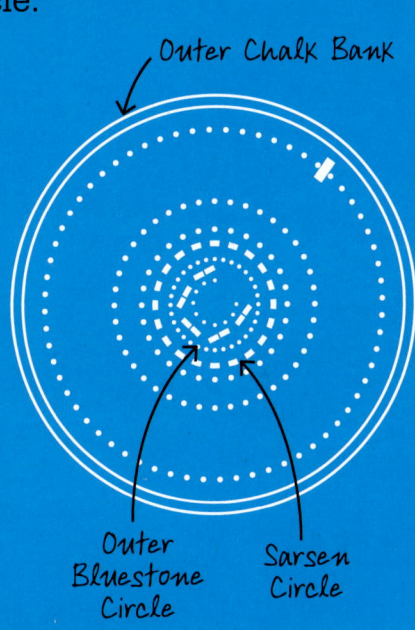

1. Find the diameter of the: a) Outer Chalk Bank b) Exterior of the Sarsen Circle c) Interior of the Sarsen Circle d) Outer Bluestone Circle.

2. Taking pi to equal 3.14, use your answers to work out the circumference for:
   a) Outer Chalk Bank
   b) Exterior of the Sarsen Circle
   c) Interior of the Sarsen Circle
   d) Outer Bluestone Circle.

3. Use a calculator to find the approximate area of the Interior of the Sarsen Circle.

Give all your answers to 1 *decimal place.*

**MISSION 12**

# GALÁPAGOS

Your final mission takes you to the wondrous Galápagos Islands, off the coast of South America, home to many rare and magnificent creatures.

### LEARN ABOUT IT
### DATA HANDLING

**When reading tables, make sure you read the row and column headings carefully.**

This table shows information on *population* changes to some of the creatures of the Galápagos. Over the centuries, the populations have gone down as humans have exploited the animals for food, and following the introduction of rats, cats and dogs. Since 1970, a breeding programme has restored some of the populations.

| Year | Estimated populations of: | | | |
|---|---|---|---|---|
| | **Blue-footed boobies** | **Iguanas** | **Tortoises** | **Sea lions** |
| **1600** | unknown | unknown | 250,000 | unknown |
| **1830** | unknown | unknown | 150,000 | 80,000 |
| **1900** | unknown | 10,000 | 50,000 | 50,000 |
| **1970** | 20,000 | 1000 | 6000 | 40,000 |
| **2014** | 6400 | 9000 | 25,000 | 10,000 |

26

On this *line graph*, each small interval on the vertical *axis* can be found by dividing 5000 by 5, so each is worth 1000. To find the population in a particular year, read up from the year to the red line and then across to the left. To find when the population was a particular size, read across from that number to the red line and then down to the year.

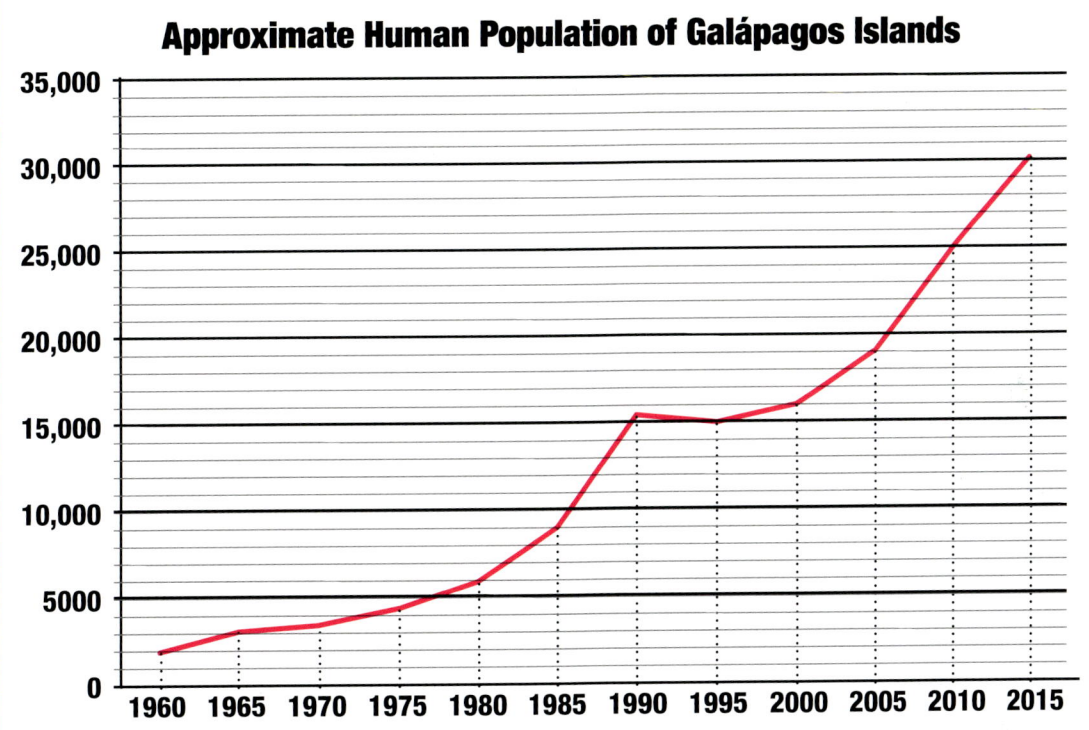

**Approximate Human Population of Galápagos Islands**

## ›GO FIGURE!

Interpret the graphs and tables to find facts and stats to include in your travel guide.

1. Due to whalers killing tortoises for food, the population of tortoises declined greatly between 1830 and 1900. By how many did it decline?

2. Sea lion numbers are strongly affected by El Niño (a weather system with warm waters). By how many did their population decline between 1970 and 2014?

3. A breeding and reintroduction program for tortoises began in 1970. What has happened to their population since?

4. Approximately how much greater is the human population in 2015 than in 1970?

27

# GO FIGURE! ANSWERS

## 04–05 The Pyramids of Egypt
1. 230.4 x 230.4 = 53,084.16 m²
   215.2 x 215.2 = 46,311.04 m²
   105.5 x 1.05.5 = 11,130.25 m²
2. 146.5 – 7.7 = 138.8 m
3. 143.5 – 65.5 = 78 m
4. (½ x 230.4 x 186.3) x 4 + 53,084.16
   = 138,931.2 m²
   (½ x 215.2 x 179.6) x 4 + 46,311.04
   = 123,610.88 m²
   (½ x 105.5 x 84.4) x 4 + 11,130.25
   = 28,938.65 m²

## 06–07 The Taj Mahal
1. Photo A shows two lines of reflective symmetry.
2. There are two full translations in the pattern.
3. Shape c is an irregular hexagon.
4. a has three lines of symmetry
   b has six lines of symmetry
   c has two lines of symmetry
5. The shape has:
   16 sides
   16 lines of reflective symmetry
   A rotational symmetry order of 16
   8 right angles
   8 obtuse angles

## 08–09 Waterfalls of the World
1. a) Angel Falls has the greatest height.
   b) Niagara Falls has the largest flow rate.
   c) Iguazu Falls has the greatest width.
2. a) Angel Falls – 980 m
      Iguazu Falls – 80 m
      Kaieteur Falls – 230 m
      Niagara Falls – 50 m
      Victoria Falls – 110 m
   b) Angel Falls – 100 m
      Iguazu Falls – 2700 m
      Kaieteur Falls – 100 m
      Niagara Falls – 1200 m
      Victoria Falls – 1700 m
3. a) 105,360 m³  b) 144,420 m³
4. Iguazu Falls scores the most points with 11, and it would still score the highest if the last two columns were included, with 18 points.

## 10–11 The Great Wall of China
1. a) Eight thousand, eight hundred and fifty kilometres
   b) Forty thousand and seventy five kilometres
   c) Twenty one thousand, one hundred and ninety six kilometres
2. a) 26.3608 million
   b) 26.2903 million
   c) 27.1916 million
3. a) One hundred and seven million, two hundred thousand
   b) 107,200,000
   c) 107.2 million
   d) 0.1072 billion

## 12–13 Terracotta Army
1. 3 x 68 = 204 soldiers
2. 9 x 36 x 4 = 1296 soldiers
3. a) 21 x 17 = 357 m²
   b) 94 x 84 = 7896 m²
   c) 210 x 62 = 13,020 m²
4. 13,020 ÷ 4 = 3255 m²

## 14–15 The Amazon
1. 17,400 x 9 = 156,600 km²
2. 19,400 – 17,400 = 2000 km²
   = 200,000 hectares
3. 19,400 – 8600 = 10,800 km²
   = 1,080,000 hectares
   and 1.08 million hectares
4. (17,400 x 9) + (19,400 x 9) + (8600 x 9)
   = 408,600 km² = 40.86 million hectares

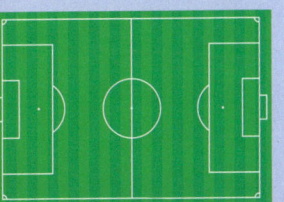

## 16–17 Antarctica
1. Mean temperature in:
   a) November = -10°C  b) January = -2°C
   c) May = -22°C  d) July = -26°C
2. January is the warmest month.
3. a) September is 14°C colder than February
   b) March is 8°C colder than November
4. The mean average temperature for whole
   year is: -2 + -10 + -18 + -20 + -22 + -24 +
   -26 + -26 + -24 + -18 + -10 + -4
   = -204 ÷ 12 = -17°C

## 18–19 The Acropolis
1. 30 divided by $\varphi$ is approximately 18.5 m
2. 18.5 divided by $\varphi$ is approximately 11.4 m
3. 11.4 divided by $\varphi$ is approximately 7.0 m

## 20–21 Burj Khalifa
1. 163 x 615 = 100,245 m or 100.245 km
2. a) 504 ÷ 6 = 84 seconds
      or 1 minute 24 seconds
   b) 504 ÷ 8 = 63 seconds
      or 1 minute 3 seconds
3. $\frac{5}{9}$(68 – 32) = 20°C

## 22–23 Mount Everest
1. a) 5310/8850 = $\frac{3}{5}$
   b) 5900/8850 = $\frac{2}{3}$
   c) 7080/8850 = $\frac{4}{5}$
   d) 7670/8850 = $\frac{13}{15}$
   e) 8260/8850 = $\frac{14}{15}$
2. a) 60%  b) 66.7%  c) 80%
   d) 86.7%  e) 93.3%
3. a) $\frac{9}{24}$ = $\frac{3}{8}$, b) $\frac{2}{24}$ = $\frac{1}{12}$
   c) $\frac{4}{24}$ = $\frac{1}{6}$, d) $\frac{6}{24}$ = $\frac{1}{4}$
4. $\frac{6}{24}$ = $\frac{1}{4}$ = 25%

## 24–25 Stonehenge
1. a) Outer Chalk Bank
      diameter = 56 x 2 = 112 m
   b) Exterior of the Sarsen Circle
      diameter = 16.5 x 2 = 33 m
   c) Interior of the Sarsen Circle
      diameter = 15.4 x 2 = 30.8 m
   d) Outer Bluestone Circle
      diameter = 12.1 x 2 = 24.2 m
2. a) 112 x 3.14 = 351.7 m
   b) 33 x 3.14 = 103.6 m
   c) 30.8 x 3.14 = 96.7 m
   d) 24.2 x 3.14 = 76.0 m
3. 3.14 x 15.4 x 15.4 = 744.7 m²

## 26–27 Galápagos
1. 150,000 – 50,000 = 100,000
2. 40,000 – 10,000 = 30,000
3. 25,000 – 6000 = 19,000 increase
4. 30,000 – 3500 = 26,500

# MATHS GLOSSARY

**ALGEBRA**
A type of mathematics that replaces numbers in equations with letters.

**AREA**
The amount of two-dimensional space covered by a shape or object. For example, the area of a rectangle is calculated by multiplying the length of one of the short sides by the length of one of the long sides.

**AXIS**
A line that is used in maths to locate a point.

**BILLION**
A thousand million.

**CIRCUMFERENCE**
The perimeter of a circle, the distance all the way around the edge.

**DIAMETER**
The widest length across a circle, passing through the centre.

**ESTIMATE**
To produce an answer that is roughly equivalent to the correct answer. Estimating usually involves rounding up or down the numbers involved.

**FACTOR**
A number that multiplies with another number to make a third number.

**HECTARE**
An area of 10,000 m$^2$.

**LINE GRAPH**
A type of graph that shows a sequence of data, connecting the values with a continuous line.

**LINE OF SYMMETRY**
A mirror line that divides a shape into two reflected halves. The lines marked are all lines of symmetry.

**MEAN**
A type of average that is calculated by adding together a collection of figures and then dividing by the number of figures. So the mean of the numbers 2, 3 and 4 is: 2 + 3 + 4 = 9/3 = 3

**MILLION**
A thousand thousand.

**NEGATIVE NUMBER**
A number that is less than zero.

**PERCENTAGE**
A percentage shows one number as a fraction of another number, given in hundredths. Each percentage point represents $\frac{1}{100}$ of the total.

**PERIMETER**
The total distance around a shape. The perimeter is calculated by adding together the lengths of all the shape's sides.

## PI
Written as π, pi is a special number that is approximately 3.1412… or 22/7. It is the relationship between the diameter and circumference of a circle.

## PHI
Written as φ, phi is approximately 1.618... and can be written exactly using the formula $\frac{1+\sqrt{5}}{2}$

## POPULATION
The number of people, or creatures, who live in a particular area, such as a town, region or country.

## POSITIVE NUMBER
A number that is greater than zero.

## PYRAMID
A three-dimensional shape whose sides are formed from triangles that meet at a point above a polygon base. The base can be a triangle, square, rectangle or any shape with three or more sides.

## RADIUS
The distance between the centre of a circle and its circumference.

## RATIO
Ratios show how one or more numbers or values is related to another. So a ratio of 2:1 shows that there are twice as many of the first value as there are of the second.

## ROUNDING
Changing a number up or down to the nearest ten, hundred or thousand. For example, 11 can be rounded down to 10, while 18 can be rounded up to 20.

## SYMMETRY
When a shape or object has parts that are the same when they are reflected or rotated.

## TRANSFORMATIONS
These are ways of changing or moving a shape. There are four main types of transformations: reflection, rotation, translation and enlargement.

# INDEX

algebra 20–21
apex 4
area 4–5, 14–15

Celsius 16, 21
circles 24–25
circumference 24–25
comparing numbers 8–9

diameter 24–25
division 13

Fahrenheit 21
formulae 20–21
fractions 22–23

geometry 18–19
golden ratio 18–19
golden rectangle 18–19

hectare 14

line graph 27

multiplication 12, 14

negative numbers 16–17
net 4–5

percentages 22–23
phi 18–19
pi 24–25
pyramid 4–5

radius 24–25
rectangle 4, 18
reflection 6
rotation 6
rounding 8

simplifying 22
symmetry 7

tables 15, 26–27
temperature 16–17
thermometers 16–17
transformations 6–7
translation 6
triangles 4–5

## WEBSITES

**www.mathisfun.com**
A huge website packed full of explanations, examples, games, puzzles, activities, worksheets and teacher resources for all age levels.

**www.bbc.co.uk/bitesize**
The revision section of the BBC website, it contains tips and easy-to-follow instructions on all subjects, including maths, as well as games and activities.

**www.mathplayground.com**
An action-packed website with maths games, mathematical word problems, worksheets, puzzles and videos.

## ACKNOWLEDGEMENTS

First published in Great Britain in 2016 by Wayland

Copyright © Wayland, 2016

All rights reserved

Editor: Elizabeth Brent

Produced by Tall Tree Ltd
Editors: Rob Colson and Joe Fullman
Designer: Ed Simkins

ISBN: 9780750297875

Wayland, an imprint of Hachette Children's Group
Part of Hodder and Stoughton
Carmelite House
50 Victoria Embankment
London EC4Y 0DZ

An Hachette UK Company
www.hachette.co.uk
www.hachettechildrens.co.uk

Printed and bound in China

10 9 8 7 6 5 4 3 2 1

The website addresses (URLs) included in this book were valid at the time of going to press. However, it is possible that contents or addresses may have changed since the publication of this book. No responsibility for any such changes can be accepted by either the author or the Publisher.

Picture credits
All istockphoto: 4-5 Ugurhan Betin, 6 turtix, 7tr ConradFries, 7br paulprescott72, 9 best-photo, 10–11 bjdlzx, 12–13 BartZuidema, 12l OliverChilds, 12r sinopics, 13b OliverChilds, 14–15 RodReis, 16–17 heckepics, 19t Emmanouil Filippou, 19b Lingbeek, 20 kjorgen, 22–23 isoft, 24–25 charmedesign, 26t MindStorm-inc, 26cl benjamint444, 26cr shalamov, 27, 31 tlindne